All about...

Malorie
Blackman

Heinemann
LIBRARY

Shaun McCarthy

www.heinemann.co.uk/library

Visit our website to find out more information about **Heinemann Library** books.

To order:

 Phone 44 (0) 1865 888066

 Send a fax to 44 (0) 1865 314091

 Visit the Heinemann Bookshop at www.heinemann.co.uk/library to browse our catalogue and order online.

First published in Great Britain by Heinemann Library, Halley Court, Jordan Hill, Oxford OX2 8EJ, part of Harcourt Education. Heinemann is a registered trademark of Harcourt Education Ltd.

Editorial: Lucy Thunder and Helen Cannons
Design: David Poole and Geoff Ward
Picture Research: Rebecca Sodergren and Kay Altwegg
Production: Edward Moore

Originated by Ambassador Litho Ltd
Printed and bound in China by South China Printing

ISBN 978 0 431 17982 7 (hardback)
07 06 05 04
10 9 8 7 6 5 4 3 2

ISBN 978 0 431 17992 6 (paperback)
08
10 9 8 7 6 5 4 3 2

British Library Cataloguing in Publication Data
McCarthy, Shaun
Blackman, Malorie. – (All About...)
823.9'14
A full catalogue record for this book is available from the British Library.

Acknowledgements
The Publishers would like to thank the following for permission to reproduce photographs: BBC p**21**; Corbis (Charles Gupton) p**15**; Corbis/Norman Parkinson Ltd (Fiona Cowan) p**11**; Corgi Press pp**20**, **24**; Mark Farrell p**29**; Frith Photos p**7**; Goldsmiths College, London p**12**; Hulton Archive p**8**; Julia Martin/Photofusion p**19**; Malorie Blackman pp**6**, **10**, **13**, **17**, **23**, **25**, **27**; Paramount Television/Ronald Grant Archive p**9**; Random House pp**5**, **18**, **26**, **28**; Rex Features p**4**; Womens Press Ltd p**16**.

Cover photograph of a publicity shot of Malorie Blackman, reproduced with permission of Random House.

Sources
The author and Publishers gratefully acknowledge the websites below which were used for research and as written sources for this book:
Achuka Authorfile and Achuka: Malorie Blackman Revisited –
www.achuka.co.uk/mbsg.htm
Amazon reader reviews – www.amazon.com
Channel Four Book Box –
www.channel4.com/bookbox
Jubilee Books – www.jubileebooks.co.uk
Our Lady of Lourdes Primary School: Malorie Blackman visit –
www.esc.lewisham.gov.uk/ololbhm/mb2.htm
Young Writer magazine –
www.mystworld.com/youngwriter

The Publishers would like to thank Stephen Noon for his assistance in the preparation of this book.

Every effort has been made to contact copyright holders of any material reproduced in this book. Any omissions will be rectified in subsequent printings if notice is given to the Publishers.

Contents

Any words shown in the text in bold, **like this**, are explained in the Glossary.

The author and Publishers would like to thank Malorie Blackman for her invaluable help in the writing of this book.

Who is Malorie Blackman?

Malorie Blackman is a very popular author of books for children and young people. She writes about all sorts of subjects, including computer **hacking**, **organ transplants**, **racism** and other complex and serious subjects. Her books have won many prizes. Two of her best-known books – *Thief* and *Pig-Heart Boy* – have been turned into successful television series. Malorie has also written lots of stories for younger readers, including the very popular *Operation Gadgetman*.

Malories smiling at the success and popularity of her many books.

Gripping reads ·

Whatever subject Malorie chooses to write about, she invents a gripping plot to keep you reading. She is very good at creating **characters** that young readers can really sympathize with, who have to face and make difficult decisions. Most of all, her books are full of energy and her own great sense of humour.

Families and friends

Many of Malorie's books are **dedicated** to members of her family. Families and relationships are important in her books. Her characters often struggle to make relationships with family and friends work. Family is a very important part of Malorie's own life.

Author of *THIEF!* and *PIG-HEART BOY*

MALORIE BLACKMAN

HACKER

WINNER OF THE YOUNG TELEGRAPH/GIMME 5 AWARD and THE WHS MIND-BOGGLING BOOKS AWARD

▲ Computers are an important part of the plot in *Hacker*, Malorie's first best-selling book.

Factfile

★ Date of birth	8 February 1962
★ Star sign	Aquarius
★ Eye colour	Brown
★ Hair colour	Black
★ Pets	Malorie is proud of all the animals she lives with: a rabbit, a frog, a leopard, several bears and monkeys, a haggis and a whale – all stuffed toys of course!
★ Hobbies	Playing musical instruments: guitar, piano, saxophone
★ Favourite food	Roast lamb and potatoes
★ Favourite Childhood book	*The Silver Chair* by C. S. Lewis.
★ Bad habit	Impatience. 'I want everything to have happened yesterday!'
★ Personal motto	'Don't give up!'

Early years

Malorie was born in 1962 in Beckenham, a **suburb** of London. Malorie's parents were from Barbados in the West Indies. Her father was a carpenter and her mother was a seamstress (skilled in making clothes). Malorie was the first of their children to be born in England. She had an older sister and brother. Two younger brothers were born later.

▲ A very young Malorie in the park near where she lived.

A happy childhood

Malorie grew up in an ordinary middle-sized house in an ordinary suburban street. There were open fireplaces with coal fires, which had to be cleaned out and lit every winter morning. She remembers the house always being busy with relations, friends and neighbours coming and going. The family had a piano, which she loved to try to play.

▲ This photo was taken in Beckenham in 1965.

Malorie remembers her mum and dad talking about their old life in Barbados a lot. They missed the warmth of the place and the people, compared to England. Her mum told Malorie that when she was little she used to play football using a mango (big round fruit) as the ball, just for a laugh!

An early reader

Her mother said that Malorie could read by the age of three, and after that she was rarely without a book in her hand. Both Malorie and her mum loved fairy stories, myths and legends. When she was not reading, Malorie would play in the nearby park in what local children called 'the woods', although it was only a tiny patch of tree-filled land. Malorie says, 'To us it was a forest, though!'

'Ignorant, nasty people'

Malorie was sometimes treated badly by people. There was **racism** at this time in the area where she lived. Sometimes she was spat at and barged off the pavement because she was a black child. She says 'I just thought of this as the actions of ignorant, nasty people. I wasn't aware of racism and so it didn't cast a shadow over my life. I just got on with enjoying myself.'

Going to school

Malorie first went to Churchfields Primary School in Beckenham, but soon transferred to Dalmain Primary School in nearby Brockley. This school had a greater mix of children from **ethnic backgrounds** than Churchfields. She got picked on during her first week, but things settled down and Malorie became a happy, though sometimes rather shy, pupil.

▲ Children playing in 1972 at a school like the one Malorie went to.

Talking too much!

Malorie says she was a normal pupil, good at English and quite good at maths. However, she admits she was always being told off for laughing and chattering. One school report said 'Malorie is prone to unnecessary outbursts of laughter'. Malorie does not think she has changed much since then – she still talks and laughs a lot!

Fairy tales and outer space

Malorie continued to love reading. One favourite book at this time was *The Silver Chair* by C. S. Lewis, part of his Narnia series of stories about a magic world.

What Malorie says

Malorie's love of English showed itself in unusual ways:

'I loved reading and writing at school and used to give myself English homework by writing stories and poems in my English workbook! My teacher didn't mind though and used to mark them anyway and give me her comments. She did make me read one of my poems out loud on parent's day, which put me off writing for a while.'

Malorie was also writing her own stories, but it never occurred to her that she could actually become a writer some day. In fact, her greatest ambition was to be the Bridge Officer responsible for steering the *Starship Enterprise*, the spaceship in the **science fiction** television series *Star Trek*! It was one of Malorie's favourite programmes when she was young, and, like many *Star Trek* fans, she still loves it now she is older.

▲ Malorie dreamed of being one of the crew of the *Starship Enterprise*.

Secondary school

When she was eleven, Malorie started at Honor Oak Grammar School in Peckham. She loved this school. She especially enjoyed English and had decided that she wanted to be a teacher herself. The school had lovely grounds around it, like a small park with a stream running through the middle. She says that 'On sunny, summer days we used to spend our lunch times jumping the stream and then laughing like crazy when anyone fell in.'

Keeping a diary

Sadly, Malorie's mother and father split up when she was thirteen. Malorie felt so upset she couldn't talk about it. She started a diary to have 'something to share my feelings and thoughts with'.

Malorie says that writing a diary is a really good way of getting into the habit of writing every day. She also says you should hide your diary where no one else can find it! That's what she did.

▲ Malorie when she was at Honor Oak School. She had to do her homework as soon as she got home each night and her parents kept a very close eye on her school reports.

True teenagers

Young readers often say they like Malorie's books because her teenage **characters** seem so real. This is probably because Malorie can clearly remember what it felt like to be a young person herself and uses this in her writing. She says, 'When I became a teenager, I believed I knew everything. The world was black and white. This was good, that was bad, this was wrong, that was right. Only when I was older did I see that a smile doesn't always mean friendship, any more than a frown means hatred.'

One of Malorie's heroes as a teenager was World champion heavyweight boxer, Mohammed Ali. He was one of the greatest boxers of all time, and a symbol to many black people of what it was possible to achieve. ▶

Malorie's black characters

Malorie always read lots at school, but found no books that featured black characters. This is why she always has a black person as the main character in her own books. However, she says she does not feel it is her 'duty' to only write about black characters:

'Most of my characters are black because I'm black, just as other authors write about white characters because they're white themselves.'

College and work

M alorie was now eighteen and preparing to take her A levels. She had decided that she wanted to be an English teacher. She applied to Goldsmiths College, which was near to where she lived, to study English and **Drama**. To be admitted, Malorie needed a reference (a letter praising her ability) from her careers teacher. The teacher thought Malorie would fail her English A level and suggested to Malorie that she should become a secretary instead. Malorie did not want to become a secretary, so she applied to be a business studies' student at a college in Huddersfield, far away from London. Her school supported this, but Malorie was not sure she was doing the right thing.

▲ Goldsmiths College in London, shown here, was where Malorie wanted to study English and Drama.

Hooked on computers

Malorie did pass her English A level, but went off to Huddersfield anyway. She liked being a student. However, the course did not suit her at all. After a few months she had to have her **appendix** out and went home to London to recover.

Malorie decided not to go back to Huddersfield and applied to Goldsmiths to do the course she had wanted in the first place. She got in, but decided to take a year off to make some money. In 1980 she got a job at a computer **software** company. She started doing things like filing papers, but got hooked on computing!

▲ Malorie when she was a student.

Hacking

Malorie used her knowledge of computers to create a gripping story in her first best-selling book, *Hacker*. Here Vicky, the main character, is trying to **hack** into a secret computer program:

"'ENTER PASSWORD' appeared on the screen. "Cross your fingers," I said. My hands hovered over the keyboard. Please let this work, I thought desperately... I typed in the password – JABBERWOCKY44. The screen cleared. Then:

WELCOME TO THE UNIVERSAL BANK DEVELOPMENT SYSTEM.

"Yeah! I'm in, I yelled.'"

A business woman

After a few months of working, Malorie gave up the idea of going to college at all. She began working with computers as a documentation assistant, writing information into computer files. Soon she became a junior **programmer**, then a programmer. Creating complex computer programs was something she found she was very good at doing. In the end, she worked in computing for ten years.

Malorie's life was not all work. At the first software company where she worked, she met another young programmer, called Neil. Malorie was nineteen. They started going out and finally got married when Malorie was in her thirties. Their first home was a two-bedroom flat in Brockley, overlooking a park called Hilly Fields.

Study and success

Malorie studied computing at evening classes. She went on to work for several different companies, gaining new skills and better and better jobs. She became a system's programmer, an assistant project manager, a project manager and finally a database manager, designing systems to store huge amounts of information.

Travelling the world

Malorie had to travel all over the world for her job. She went to Geneva in Switzerland, Oslo in Norway, Dallas and New York in the USA, and Toronto in Canada. At first the travelling was fun, but she says that after a while 'one hotel room seems just like any other'.

▲ If she had not become a writer, Malorie might have spent all of her working life in an office like this.

Malorie now enjoyed the comfortable life style of a successful young business woman. She was designing computer software for banks and financial companies who did 'million pound deals' every day. Some people might think this an exciting job, but Malorie was realizing that the world of finance was not her thing. She wanted to do something more creative. She wanted to write.

Writing and working

Malorie started writing short stories in 1988. She would go to work all day and then come home and write until about midnight, with only a break for dinner. She was writing **science fiction** stories for adults, not children. She managed to combine work and writing like this for over two years.

I'm going to be a writer!

Malorie started sending out her finished stories to **publishers**. It was not long before one said they liked her work. In 1990, they published *Not So Stupid!*, a collection of her short stories for teenagers. It included horror, fantasy and **science fiction**, and Malorie was very proud of the book.

After that things quickly took off. She was asked to produce a picture book called *That New Dress* and another book of stories called *Girl Wonder and the Terrific Twins*. This was an illustrated story book for younger readers. When this second book of stories was accepted for publication, Malorie began to think about changing her life.

Malorie's first book was a collection of stories for teenagers.

Malorie, early on in the back bedroom where she has sat and written for many years. This was certainly a bit different from flying to computer offices all round the world!

A full-time writer

In 1991 Malorie decided she would try writing full-time for a year to see if she could make enough money from it. She gave up her job in computing and turned the back bedroom of her house into a work room where she could write her books.

What Malorie says

Malorie's early efforts at writing were not always encouraged.

'When I started writing a couple of people in my family told me I was wasting my time, I shouldn't bother... They said I would never get published. They said "There aren't any black writers"!'

Malorie says that in her first few years as a full-time writer, she wrote in every spare moment. 'It was great! I got a lot of criticism for being too prolific – writing too many books! – around this time. I did nothing but write.'

Malorie decided she wanted to write books for children of all different ages. She also decided to make the main **characters** in her books black. She was determined that young people should not feel like she did when she was young, never having the chance to read any books that had black people in them.

Books take off!

During this busy time, Malorie started writing *Hacker*. It was a book about a girl whose father is accused of stealing £1 million from the bank where he works. The girl uses her computer skills to **hack** into the bank's computers to try to prove his innocence. Malorie put her own knowledge of computers to good use in this story.

▲ Malorie holding The Young Telegraph/Gimme5 Award award for *Hacker*.

Hacker was Malorie's first attempt at a full-length **novel**. She wanted to see if she could write a story of at least 200 pages. (The paperback edition of *Hacker* is exactly 200 pages!) She started writing the story without any planning or plotting.

Novels are hard work!

When she finished *Hacker*, Malorie sent it off to her **publishers**. They were very encouraging, but sent the book back for rewriting because they did not think the plot of the story worked. Malorie reread her book, realized that the publishers were right and started again! This time she worked out the whole plot and planned what would happen in each chapter. Then she spent almost a year rewriting the story.

Hacker was finally **published** in 1992. It became her first best-seller and won two children's book awards – Malorie had made it!

▲ Like busy families everywhere, Malorie would take her daughter, Elizabeth, to nursery or school every day.

A daughter

Malorie was now writing flat out. She found she had to have complete quiet to work and she planned to write three books a year! But in 1995 Malorie had a baby daughter and for a while this peace and quiet was broken.

What Malorie says

The birth of her daughter, Elizabeth, changed Malorie's daily work routine. This is how she described her life when Elizabeth was younger:

'Take my daughter to nursery, write, collect my daughter, spend the evening with my family, write, bed. If I'm lucky I'll get in maybe four or five hours of writing a day.'

More books

Despite having a lot to do looking after Elizabeth, having a child did not prevent Malorie from writing lots more successful books. *Thief, A.N.T.I.D.O.T.E, Pig-Heart Boy, Dangerous Reality* and *Operation Gadgetman* were all written and published between 1995 and 2000. Malorie says she likes to challenge herself by writing in different styles for various ages and abilities, from very young beginner readers to teenagers.

All sorts of subjects

Malorie picked a new subject for each book. Some of her books used ideas from **science fiction**, like time travel in *Thief*, and virtual reality in *Dangerous Reality*. Other books used ideas that were very much part of the real world, like **organ transplants** in *Pig-Heart Boy* and computers in *A.N.T.I.D.O.T.E.*

Many people thought that the subject of organ transplants was too difficult for a children's book, but Malorie used it to create a gripping story in *Pig-Heart Boy*.

What readers say

Here is how one reader described what they liked about *Pig-Heart Boy*:

'What I liked was that every time something happened you knew what people were thinking about it, and how they felt ... It makes you feel like a part of the story as it unfolds around you as you read.'

(From Amazon books reader reviews)

TV successes

In 1999, Malorie had an exciting offer. BBC television in London said they wanted to turn two of Malorie's books – *Thief* and *Pig-Heart Boy* – into television **dramas**.

▲ A scene from the BBC television version of *Pig-Heart Boy*.

Malorie made sure she was involved with the TV dramas. She wrote four of the episodes of the television version of *Pig-Heart Boy* herself. Authors who have written books do not always have much to do with the **script** version that is written when their book is turned into a film or a television programme. Malorie liked visiting the set (the specially built place where scenes are filmed), even though it was quite boring sitting about while cameras and lights were set up.

One of Malorie's plans for the future is to write more scripts for TV and films. She is obviously good at it – *Pig-Heart Boy* won an award for Best Children's Drama in 2000.

A busy author

By the year 2000, Malorie was a famous children's writer and a busy mother, too. In 2001 she **published** her **novel** for young adults – *Noughts and Crosses*. It is a story about two young people who fall in love, but who are from different sides of a society divided by apartheid. This is a system where people living in the same country are divided into groups according to the colour of their skin. In real life, apartheid systems have always put white people in control of black people. But in the world Malorie creates in *Noughts and Crosses*, she has black people controlling white. Once again, she had used her imagination to create an unusual and gripping story. Others agreed! This book won the Children's Book Award in 2002.

What Benjamin Zephaniah (poet) says

'[Noughts and Crosses] must be the most original book I've ever read. It's intelligent, emotional, and imaginatively wicked.'

Malorie's tips

These are Malorie's tips for writing a great story:

1. Start with a simple idea for the plot.

2. Make the **characters** believable by writing about each one – including their appearance, their likes, dislikes and so on.

3. Make sure the story is exactly the sort of thing that you can imagine happening to these characters.

4. Make a plan of what will basically happen in each chapter.

5. Know where the plot is going by working out the beginning, middle and end.

Visiting writer

Most children's writers make regular trips to schools, bookshops and libraries to meet their readers, to sign copies of their books and talk about how they write their stories. Malorie enjoys visiting schools to meet young fans. She answers their questions on everything, from where she gets ideas for new stories to what her favourite television programme is. (*Frasier*, the US comedy show – apart from old episodes of *Star Trek,* of course!')

When a new book is published she visits bookshops to meet her fans and sign copies of the new book for them. She also does interviews for magazines. But, being a hard-working author, she spends most of her days at home writing in her back bedroom.

▲ Malorie with fans at the Word Festival at the Polka Theatre, London, in 2002.

Malorie Blackman on Malorie Blackman

Here are some of Malorie's answers to questions we asked her:

How long does it take you to write a full-length book?
  'It usually takes between five and eight months.'

Which of your own books is your favourite?
  'I've written 37 books, but I'd say *Pig-Heart Boy* and *Hacker* are my favourites.'

How do you start a new book?
  'I start with a title and the basic plot. I spend most of the time after that thinking about my **characters**. Characters make the story. I love writing 'Chapter One' and then getting down to it, just to see what comes out of my head!'

Thief was another prize-winning book. It won the Daily Telegraph Young Telegraph *Fully Booked Award* in 1995. ▶

Winner of the Young Telegraph/Fully Booked award

Pig-Heart Boy

In her book *Pig-Heart Boy*, Malorie tells the story of Cameron, a thirteen-year-old boy who needs a heart transplant and is given the heart of a pig. Here he dreams of leaving hospital:

'I slouched back against my pillows, disappointed. All I wanted to do now was go home, then go to school and show all my friends that I was the same as them. I wanted to play and swim and dance.'

Do you have to do a lot of research for your books?
'It depends on the subject matter. Books like *Pig-Heart Boy* and *Noughts and Crosses* did require research, however – especially *Pig-Heart Boy*. I did most of my research for that on the Internet, which had all the up-to-date information about everything I required. I also visited my local library, and used my own books, and so on.'

Where do you get ideas for stories from?
'Anywhere! The news, things I read, things that I hear people say.'

What exactly do you do when you go out and meet your 'fans'?
'I visit schools and libraries to talk about what it's like to be a writer. I also take creative writing classes in schools, and that can be great fun. I don't get the children to worry about adjectives and parts of speech. I'm more interested in exercises that get children and young adults using their imaginations and writing from the heart as well as the head. Because I'm on the daily 'school run' for my young daughter, most of my visits these days tend to be in London, close to where I live.'

▲ Malorie winning a book award in 2002 for *Noughts and Crosses*. The judges were children, and some of them are shown here.

Any particular memories of visits you have made to schools?

'I once went to a school and the teacher proudly informed me that they had a big selection of my books to sell afterwards. She showed me the tables that were covered with Terence Blacker's *Ms Wiz* books. When I pointed out that my name was Malorie not Terence, she was very embarrassed!'

Isn't being a writer rather a lonely job?

'I see other writers at various events and functions and belong to a black women's writers' group, but of course writing is something that you mostly do alone. I like my own company, luckily, or I'd drive myself nuts!'

Does being a successful writer mean you have an exciting and wealthy way of life?

'No, I don't drive a Bentley or anything like it. I drive a Toyota car, which is giving me a great deal of trouble at the moment!!'

Malorie, the hard-working writer who enjoys her own company.

Malorie enjoys playing the piano to relax. ▶

What do you do to relax when you've finished writing for the day?
'I play computer games. And I read. We have over 10,000 books in the house (at the last count)! I'm having piano lessons at the moment. I love music so I thought I should learn to play at least one instrument properly.'

Do you have a favourite place to read?
'No, I'll read in bed, or in the bath, or on a train, in the living room – anywhere.'

Do you have a special time for writing each day?
'Yes. On working days I write between ten in the morning and about twenty to five in the afternoon.'

Do you believe in ghosts, like the one you wrote about in your book Grandma Gertie's Handbag?
'I believe that sometimes when we die we might leave something of ourselves behind, so yes I guess I do believe in ghosts. I've never seen one, though.'

Doing a job she loves

Malorie is always busy with exciting ideas for new books. She had two very different books **published** in 2002. *Jessica Strange* is an illustrated book for young readers, about a farmyard mouse who is not sure that she is actually a mouse. ('Some animals say she's a cow, others think she might be an ant!') Her other new book, *Dead Gorgeous*, is very different again. It is about an eleven-year-old girl whose parents buy a run-down hotel that is haunted by the ghost of a 'gorgeous' teenage boy. Malorie says she is now planning another book about a future world 'and not a very nice one either!'

MALORIE BLACKMAN

Dead Gorgeous

Why write?

Malorie says the main reason she started writing stories for children was because of the lack of books for young people in the UK featuring black **characters** and written by black writers. For many readers, Malorie was the first to create popular children's books with black main characters.

Malorie's new book for young adult readers.

Just a writer

Malorie says that now, when she is sitting in front of her computer, she's just a professional and popular writer trying to write books that will appeal to, thrill and entertain anyone who likes reading. Many fans will agree that her books certainly do that.

Malorie is a successful author, but she often tells children in the schools she visits not to rush into writing. She says 'I'd recommend writing as a good life, but only after living a life first. It's a good job to come to after you've done other things and other jobs.'

And she says – after all this – she still wants to be Bridge Officer on the Starship Enterprise!

▲ Malorie's many books can be found in the children's section of bookshops.

What Malorie says

'I feel very lucky to be a writer. I'm doing a job I love and I can't imagine doing anything else. I'll never stop writing. I hope when I drop dead I'm found at my computer, or at least with a pen in my hand!'

Timeline

1962 Malorie Blackman is born in Beckenham, London

1980 She starts work in the computer industry

1990 *Not So Stupid*, Malorie's first book, is **published**

1992 *Hacker*, her first successful full-length **novel** for children is published. Malorie gives up computer career to be a full-time writer.

1994 *Hacker* wins Young Telegraph Children's Book of the Year Award

1995 Malorie's daughter, Elizabeth, is born

1996 *Thief*, another of her successful books, wins the Daily Telegraph Fully Booked Award

1997 *Pig-Heart Boy* is published

1998 *Pig-Heart Boy* is made into a television series (shown on TV in 1999)

2001 *Noughts and Crosses*, her first novel for young adults is published

Books by Malorie Blackman

Here are some books by Malorie you might like to read:

Hacker (first published in 1992)
When Vicky's father is accused of stealing over a million pounds from the bank where he works, she is determined to prove his innocence by **hacking** into the bank's computer system...

Thief! (first published in 1995)
A silly dare – to take a school cup and keep it over night – turns into a time-travelling adventure into a very scary future world.

Pig-Heart Boy (first published in 1997)
A thirteen-year-old boy is in desperate need of a heart transplant operation. The surgeon cannot give him a replacement human heart, but he can give him one from a pig...

Glossary

appendix small organ of the human body, part of the intestine. If it causes pain it may be removed.

characters people in a story

dedicate when an author names someone that is special to them at the front of a book

drama story written as a script to be performed as a play or as a film or television programme

ethnic background a person's race or the culture that they grew up in

hack to use computer skills to break into other people's private computer files

information technology name for computers, computer programs and the Internet

novel a book-length story

organ transplant very complex operation where a damaged or diseased organ in the human body is replaced with a healthy one

programmer someone who invents software programs for computers

publish when someone's writing is printed as a book

publishers company that makes and sells books

racism treating people who are from a different ethnic background unfairly or even violently

science fiction type of story, usually about future or fantasy worlds, or set in space, using lots of ideas from science, computers and so on

script story written down mainly as words to be spoken for a play, film or television programme

software computer programmes, anything from word processing to games

suburb neighbourhood (with houses, schools and few local shops) at the edge of a big town, where it is less noisy and busy

Index